AMETHYST BEACH

Meditations

Barbara Merritt

SKINNER HOUSE BOOKS

BOSTON

Printed in the United States.

Cover design by Kathryn Sky-Peck
Text design by Suzanne Morgan

ISBN 1-55896-522-X
978-1-55896-522-5

Library of Congress Cataloging-in-Publication Data

Merritt, Barbara.
  Amethyst Beach : meditations / Barbara Merritt.
    p. cm.
  ISBN-13: 978-1-55896-522-5 (pbk. : alk. paper)
  ISBN-10: 1-55896-522-X (pbk. : alk. paper) 1. Meditations. 2. Unitarian Universalist Association—Prayers and devotions. I. Title.

BX9855.M47 2007
242—dc22

                    2007004298

My husband, Jeffrey, and my sons, Robert and David, have taught me almost everything I know about laughter and love. Trish Dougherty, Dorothy Green, Donna Rossio, and Barbara Foley helped shape these essays. Reverends Nancy Bowen, Forrest Church, Dick Sparrow, and John Buehrens told me to keep writing. Stacey Coates, Melissa Blacker, and Dr. Bill Fortier have been physicians to my heart, mind, and soul. Mary Benard and Marshall Hawkins at Skinner House Books have sharpened the prose. Finally, I gratefully acknowledge my spiritual teacher, Maharaj Charan Singh, who taught me that every child of God is loved and that there is a way home.

—Barbara Merritt

Contents

Amethyst Beach

The Canadian dollar exchange was so attractive this summer that the Merritt family decided to cross the Bay of Fundy and explore the opposite shore of Nova Scotia. We boarded our ship in St. John's, New Brunswick, and arrived in less than three hours. We drove forever, found an inn in a tiny village, and spent the night. When we were ready to depart the next morning, I noticed several pieces of natural amethyst for sale in the innkeeper's gift shop. I mentioned to her that the Canadian Tourist literature had made a reference to an "amethyst beach," where you could collect your own. She smiled delightedly and explained that this famous beach was their village beach, only five minutes away.

She not only gave us directions to Sandy Beach, which was down several local unmarked roads, she also gave us a quick course on "amethyst hunting." She told us to look for the boulders of black volcanic rock. On the surface of those rocks, we'd find white lines, the cracks where the crystals form. When we could locate the larger cavities of crystals, we'd be harvesting amethyst.

I'm unsure whether my children, the rock hounds, were more excited than the adults. We brought along a large canvas bag to haul back all of our semiprecious gemstones.

We found the beach with the black smooth volcanic rock and the white lines. Using our hammers and safety goggles, we went to work.

An hour later we were still smashing at rocks for no apparent reason. Deep within the white crystal cracks, we discovered a lot of rock, but no amethyst.

Initially I scanned the boulders for visual clues for hidden caches of amethyst. I'd make a thoughtful scientific appraisal of the area, following fault lines, looking for subtle gradations in color, listening for hollow echoes with my hammer. At each spot where I initially chose to chip away, my hopes were high. I was sure that this was it. It wasn't.

Later I decided to use my intuition. I "opened" myself to the presence of amethyst; I tried to become emotionally in tune with the geological harmony of the place. I attempted to be "guided" to the right spot. When everything felt "just right," I'd strike with the hammer. And lo and behold, underneath the surface, were more rocks.

One can expectantly smash rocks on a beach for only so long. My husband and children had fared no better than I had. In our initial attempts, we had each made premature declarations that we were about to break open the mother lode of amethyst.

The canvas sack remained empty.

Then, on the horizon, a man approached who looked like he knew what he was doing. We casually walked over, and he patiently explained the secrets for finding amethysts. He had all the right equipment and maps. An expert! Our hopes soared once more, and we watched in admiration as he showed us exactly where he expected to find the jewels. He hammered away, and in the white crack he broke open, he uncovered a lot more rocks, identical to the ones on the surface.

As we were leaving the beach, with my still empty canvas bag, I saw out of the corner of my eye, a small piece of black rock. I picked it up, turned it over, and I saw it—a faint pinkish cast to the crystals. I tucked it in my pocket and went on my way.

I have heard that when something is valuable and worthwhile, you are not apt to find it lying around in great heaps. Diamonds and gold are rare. Lions do not congregate in large numbers. God is not easy to find. Truth is not easy to put your hands on. But the saints, in all religious traditions, say that there is something about the search itself that instructs us, humbles us, and informs us. Our own lives sometimes appear to be empty of spiritual treasure but this doesn't mean that treasure doesn't exist. People do find amethysts. People do experience the reality of God. Having spent a little time on Amethyst Beach, I suspect that the ones who "find" are the ones who never give up the search.

Hiding the Mess

About six cups of raw oats fell on the kitchen floor. The top had been left off the box, and the cascade of grain was impressive. I had gotten out the broom and the dustpan and started to sweep it up, when my four-year-old asked if he could have the job. I said, "Sure," and went on making the coffee. A minute later I looked around and saw, to my amazement, that he was studiously pushing small piles of the oats under the refrigerator, into the fireplace, and under the counters.

I screamed, "No! That's not how you sweep up oats! Put them in the dustpan." And he quietly replied that he had been "hiding" the oats. When hearing my story, my brother-in-law's only comment was, "That nut didn't fall far from the tree."

True. I have been known to "clean up the living room" by gathering up the piles of mail and books and putting them in the dining room. I have "shut doors" when company was coming rather than take the time to make a room presentable.

But later that day, I found that the instinct to "hide the mess" goes deeper than that. I was at the hairdresser, and I explained to her that I was a nervous wreck about an upcoming speech. I wanted her to give me a haircut that made me look "cool, composed, and in control." I was hoping that the right coiffure might effectively hide my anxiety level.

Then my back went out. My doctor suggested that it might have something to do with the stress level I was carrying around about the speech. I told him in no uncertain terms that this was a ridiculous idea. My back went out because I lifted a mattress the wrong way! (How surprised I was to discover that, immediately after the speech, my back felt perfectly fine. Even my body knows how to hide its pain away.)

The messy side of life is normal, healthy, and part of the creative process. Nature itself is wonderfully messy. Observe the pollen and the stringy stuff that fall out of maple trees in the springtime. Daffodils are glorious but look rather bedraggled in late spring. Not all of life is pristine, beautiful, and orderly. Neither are we.

It's all right to hide the mess from the general public. Emotional overexposure is culturally fashionable at the moment, but it does not necessarily contribute to the common good. Everyone does not need to know everything. But we shouldn't have to hide the mess from ourselves or from the people who love us. Because in what we call "the mess," creation itself is at work. This universe, our universe, is a place of life, growth, change, spilled oats, and great confusion. And out of that odd combination, the human spirit grows.

Feeding the Pit

Part of the advantage of having an elevator being installed two feet from my office door is that I can easily listen in on the construction crew's conversation. It echoes up from two floors below. It rings down the hallway. And in between the drilling, the chain-rattling, the pounding, and the sawing, comes some helpful theological reflection.

This particular conversation occurred between a man who was balanced on a forty-five-degree ladder over a three-story, open elevator pit, and the man assisting him. The man on the ladder, who gave me a greater appreciation for having been called to the ministry, asked for four bolts. His colleague said, and I quote, "I'll give you five; you need to have one to feed the pit."

Now I can only surmise that this wisdom had been hard won. People who work over great cavities of open air have probably learned through experience about gravity. Objects fall. They will fall a great distance when there is nothing to stop them. Ergo: If you are going to suspend yourself over a deep pit, don't assume that everything will go perfectly. Don't assume that a nut or a bolt won't roll away. Assume that additional resources will come in handy. Acknowledge the challenging nature of the assignment. Take a relationship with the pit where you willingly and gracefully accept that it will occasionally need to be fed.

The alternative is simply too costly. To assume that things will go smoothly—that hammers won't drop, that nails won't bend, that parts won't wander—is to place yourself in special danger. Especially when your workplace is at the top of a ladder suspended over a fifty-foot drop.

Pits are real. Some places in human existence pose genuine danger. Illness, conflict, and accidents can quickly take everything we hold as precious.

Some people advise, "Don't look down. Pretend that nothing bad could ever happen to you or anyone you love." This is the "Ignore the Pit" school.

Another popular option is to "Decry the Pit." "Isn't it terrible that there are pits in this world?" "Ain't it awful that I have fallen in?"

Many allegedly smart people have spent their entire lives arguing about why pits exist and justifying how offended and angry they are that dangerous places continue to exist.

Some become profoundly cynical when they discover how painful a pit fall can be. "What's the use?" they sigh. "With so much destruction and unhappiness in the past, and so much possible misery in the future, why build at all?" They become paralyzed with fear.

At the moment, I am drawn to the simple teaching of the elevator man. "Feed the Pit." Right from the beginning, I should expect to encounter danger, demons, difficulties, and delays on the journey. We need to build a generous contingency fund into every life plan; and carry a few extra rations of energy, kindness, and hope in our pockets to offer to an unpredictable and hungry world.

Tampering

It is hard to write or think with a car siren wailing in the background. Indeed, it was hard for any of the staff to get any work done one morning, when a small pickup truck, illegally parked under the window of the church office, started screaming.

When I say "screaming," I am not just referring to the irritating noise that an alarm siren makes, over and over again. No, this car also talked in a harsh, machine-generated, nasal voice. After two short blasts of an ear-piercing siren, it then announced to a city block, "I've been tampered with! I've been tampered with!" Then immediately, two more short blasts and a replay of the verbal message.

At 9:15 we desperately called the towing company. They told us they couldn't tow that particular kind of vehicle because of the way it was parked. By 10:00, I suggested we just "shoot the car, and put it out of its misery." By 11:00, I started talking back to the pickup truck in a threatening manner. "So you think you've been tampered with? I'll show you what real tampering looks like."

By noon, we threw up our hands and went to lunch. Apparently so did the owner of the pickup truck, because by 1:00, the car was gone, and the parking lot was filled with blissful silence.

Halfway through the noisy ordeal, it occurred to me that I have known many people who, when nudged, begin their version of "I've been tampered with!" What you hear, with even the slightest of contact, is a laundry list of complaints, recriminations, and accusations. Soon after this insight, I admitted that I, myself, when nudged, have been known to come up with a quite elaborate litany of major and minor grievances.

When you hear a car scream over and over, "I've been tampered with!" one response is, "Well, who among us hasn't been?" All of us on the road get bumped, jostled, and dented.

Expectation has something to do with it. If you assume that life will be a painless affair, then even the slightest jar or disappointment will come as a rude shock. If you assume that spirituality or religion will cure all your health problems, will harmonize your family dynamics, will improve your financial portfolio, and change your personality, then when reality comes roaring in, you're going to feel that religion has failed you.

The life of the spirit is too demanding, too rigorous, to allow for meekness, helplessness, fragility, or sentimentality. If we wish to endure, if we wish to experience the love of God and the love of our fellow human beings, then we're going to have to roll up our sleeves, get to work, and develop some resiliency. We might as well get used to the idea that along the way our plans will be tampered with, our risks will be substantial, and our courage will be required.

Halloween Standards

✍

My son Robbie insisted on being a dinosaur this Halloween, but the only one worth being was a Tyrannosaurus rex. More specifically, a purple Tyrannosaurus rex. The day of Halloween was completely reserved for the project. We went to the fabric store and found a nice shiny purple material.

That afternoon the sewing machine and I had one of our very infrequent encounters. I made a small but wide pair of purple pants. The cape had a robust tail that stood out a good foot and a half. I taped some old quilt batting to my son's bicycle helmet and then covered it with purple cloth to make the large reptilian head. We painted some jagged teeth on my son's smiling face. There he stood—a purple Tyrannosaurus rex. I admit that I was anxious when we finally assembled the components of the costume, but I was ultimately pleased with the result.

Off we went to "trick or treat," with me glancing frequently at my son. I was admiring my own handiwork. I should have been forewarned when my husband declared that Robbie looked more like an alien than "the king of the tyrant lizards." I should have been suspicious when absolutely no one guessed what he was. But I was utterly unprepared for the fact that at four separate households, the hostess dispensing candy asked whether or not he was an eggplant.

An eggplant!

I have since concluded that it was all a matter of expectations. I, who have very minimal skills as a seamstress, was delighted that I had made a costume at all. I was even more excited that the tail didn't drag and that the head was large enough. I had met and surpassed my own standards. But apparently I did not come up to the costuming standards of the Halloween public. I had fallen short of their conception of what a tyrannosaurus would look like. My standards and theirs were different.

It can be just as painful when public standards are lower than your own. Everyone can be pleased and applaud your work, but if you have not met your own expectations of excellence, no one can convince you that you have not failed. I have known some phenomenally successful people who, because of some stern inner judge, could never feel as if they had succeeded.

But remember that the public does not always make the correct assessment. Sometimes the world is lacking in imagination, in understanding, in capacities to interpret the creative vision. No matter what your standards, please bear in mind that not every small, shiny purple person who walks by on Halloween night is an eggplant.

It's Time Somebody Told You

Now I'm not one for "affirmations." Saying something doesn't make it so. But recently a dear friend of mine read to me some affecting lines from an unknown author. They went something like this:

It's time somebody told you that you are lovely, good and real; that your beauty can make hearts stand still. It's time somebody told you how much they love and need you, how much your spirit helped set them free, how your eyes shine full of light. It's time somebody told you.

As these words were read, I found a very complex internal process going on within me. I was touched, unnerved, and a little sad that I hadn't heard these words as a child. But mostly I became conscious of enormous resistance. Something in me was not ready to let these words in. It could be that I was not quite ready to hear such positive feedback. Maybe it wasn't yet the right time to receive love and affection. But apparently, at least one friend thought that now was a good time to attend to what is essential and life-giving. Often we are too busy, too distracted, to listen to what our loved ones have to tell us. They offer all kinds of radical and startling opinions about our place in the divine scheme of things. Messages that I can almost hear include:

"It's time someone told you that with all your flaws and weaknesses, you are an extraordinary person, well-worth knowing. No one—especially not God or the people who love you—expects you to live without making mistakes or stumbling occasionally. It's time you looked at your own life with more kindness, gentleness, and mercy."

"It's time someone told you that you are not on this earth to impress anyone, to dazzle us with your success, to conquer all obstacles with your competence, or to offer one brilliant solution after another. We are happy you are here with the rest of us struggling souls. We are all striving to be as faithful as we can be to the truth that we understand. No more is required."

"It's time someone told you that the work you do to increase your capacity to love and to pay attention is more important than any other activity. As you advance closer to what is ultimately true and life-giving, you bless others."

"It's time somebody told you how absolutely beautiful your laughter is. You bring joy into our world."

Just possibly, messages of love and acceptance have always been circulating in our midst. The hard part is not seeking out these positive and creative affirmations that remind us that we are loved. The hard part is taking in the love.

It's time someone told us all that we are valued and infinitely worthwhile.

And it's time we believed it.

Dirt Farming

When Jesus told his parable of the sower and the seed, he gave very specific warnings about the dangers of planting in untilled soil, rocky soil, and soil with weeds and thorns. But he never mentioned the folly of attempting to farm in clay soil. Probably because from time immemorial, it has been obvious to everyone that clay is not conducive to green and growing things.

Except to the Merritts.

We keep trying to grow grass. In clay.

A large granite ledge that caps the hill behind our house ends halfway across our backyard. The water that drains off that rock carries silt and clay, and almost gives us an underground watering system. The dirt that has accumulated at the bottom of the hill resembles porcelain. It has a fine, sticky, slick feel, probably perfect for making pots.

I bought a book about lawns for the agriculturally challenged, and it claimed that the secret to a green velvety lawn was good soil. So I have become a dirt farmer. My family and I have been working the earth. We have rototilled several times. We have raked. We have harvested stones and boulders. We have added everything the experts suggested, and then some. We have worked gypsum into the soil—and manure, topsoil, vermiculite, lime, and more peat moss than I thought existed in the

Northern Hemisphere. I even bought some cocoa shells to throw under the bushes. It smells just like hot chocolate! So even if our garden never looks good, it will smell good.

My husband finally suggested that I just throw quarters into the ground, but then he can be quite cynical.

After raking, tilling, and breaking up the soil for two solid weeks, we put in the grass seed and starter fertilizer. The manual insisted that the next step was to roll the lawn with a special barrel device. This was to insure good contact between the seed and the dirt. So everything got patted down to a nice smooth surface. In retrospect, I wonder about the wisdom of pressing down soil that has a substantial clay content. After loosening all that dirt, was it really necessary to go and compress it?

The seed instructions claim five to twenty-one days for germination. At day seven and counting, not a single green blade has emerged.

Everyone gets their own share of "bad soil" in life. The ground of our being is always a mix of gift and limitation. Some are hampered by the historical circumstances of place and time. Some have to contend with personal tragedy and loss. Some of us suffer from character flaws or temperaments that are difficult for others to work with, let alone for us to live with. And to many souls come illness, poverty, and dishonor.

We are all gardeners of the spirit. Some of us can grow grass. Some of us cannot. But I feel called to try. And that is something.

Excess Baggage

On our way to Maine one summer, my older son and I found ourselves following one of the most ridiculous looking cars I have ever seen. It was a sports utility vehicle, laden with all the evidence of American consumerism and conspicuous consumption. Lashed onto the top were a canoe and a kayak. Strapped onto the back bumper were four bicycles. Golf clubs, tennis rackets, and camping equipment were visible through the Jeep's back window. Every car that passed by stared in astonishment at this visible study in recreational excess.

The thing I found most remarkable about the vehicle in front of us was that we owned it. My husband and younger son were driving our Jeep up to Maine and we followed. After staring at our car for some miles, and noticing the attention it was attracting from drivers-by, I decided that this was an auspicious moment to have a discussion with my older child about "nonmaterialism." I explained, trying to keep a straight face, that his father and I were dedicated to an ethic of simplicity, diminishing consumption, and intentional reduction in material accumulation.

My son greeted this pronouncement with hysterical laughter. Even I had to chuckle. But I was persistent, and after his raucous laughter subsided, I explained how, throughout our married life we had, both of us, consistently chosen jobs that paid less, even when we were offered positions that paid more;

how we had invested our modest resources into education and travel rather than in real estate and furniture; and how we tried constantly to decrease our dependence and reliance on material wealth. Notwithstanding the visual evidence to the contrary, we were working to simplify our lifestyle.

Robert listened to everything I said, and then he replied, "I understand Mom. You and Dad are nonmaterialistic. You just aren't very good at it."

The Death of Li'l Anthrax

My oldest son, upon entering college, got a pet. I was appalled by his choice—a dwarf albino hamster. I have a phobia about mice. Full blown. We're talking irrational terror. And a dwarf albino hamster looks exactly like a mouse, only without a tail. So to even see this creature made me hyperventilate. Purchased in September 2001, in the midst of all kinds of predictions about biological warfare, Robert named the tiny hamster "Anthrax."

A more vicious little creature you could hardly imagine. With his sharp, little teeth, he bit everyone who put their hand in his cage. He was so fierce that he provided endless amusement, as one college student after another tried to tame him. He would have none of it! Not this hamster! Not li'l Anthrax! Human beings were the enemy and he furiously guarded his cage from any intrusion. His beady little red eyes were always on the lookout for anyone foolish enough to disturb the nest.

I began to feel some concern for the little creature during its occasional visit to our home. I bought him a larger cage and a mouse run that had plenty of warrens and chutes to explore. I found a soft old sock for him to sleep in. I would visit him in Robert's room, just to make sure he was OK. Alright, I'll admit it—I even talked to Anthrax. But I didn't touch him. And I didn't like him. He always just looked like a mouse to me. But then the fateful day came when I checked on him and felt a wave of fear. There was no movement in his cage. He had passed on.

Here is the surprise. I was quite sad that Anthrax had died! Robert was more philosophical about it. He thought that the existence of a dwarf albino hamster was somewhat miserable, even in the best of circumstances. But he also was sad when he saw his hamster all curled up and no longer biting anyone. A tiny creature, with a highly aggressive, fearful temperament, incapable of affection, emotional responsiveness, or very much learning was, nevertheless, mourned.

One of the worst ideas to ever emerge from liberal religion, in general, and Unitarianism, in particular, was the concept of "salvation by character." Eloquently championed by William Ellery Channing, this faith in excellence was embraced by those who believed in the perfectibility of human nature and the rational conquest of life's most troubling aspects. "Salvation by character" meant we were going to be so good, so charitable, so wise, and so admirable that there would be little need for grace or mercy.

Li'l Anthrax has taught me something different. Something important. Being loved has nothing to do with character. Anthrax was unapproachable and never gave anything to anyone. But he was alive, and he needed help. Our characters are complex, contradictory, and layered with strength and weakness. But love doesn't concern itself with the perfection of our personality or our resume. Love sees past the small flaws and the large ones.

"Every creature, great and small, the Lord God loves them all."

Cougars and Tigers

Rumi, the thirteenth-century Persian poet, had a way of getting to the heart of an issue, using very few words. He wrote, "If you believe that your needs can be met, and your wanting satisfied from the outside, you are really a tiger or a cougar."

Well! Rumi has some nerve. Calling us animals of prey. Just because what we want from other people or our work makes us demanding, aggressive, and manipulative?

The image is a startling one. On soft paws we slowly and stealthily circle our spouse, our partner, our child, our friend. Our hunger is immense. When we pounce, we growl, "Make me happy! Make me believe my world is purposeful, affirming, well ordered, and rewarding! Meet my needs!"

We don't just ask the people closest to us to fill us up. We go to the movies, expecting that the entertainment industry will make us laugh, cry, and feel whole. We haunt the video stores, scanning the shelves with the hope that we can locate a great film that can nourish us at home. We watch the Super Bowl, and the quality—and the not-so-quality—TV, desperately wanting to see something "good." We go to the mall, pursuing the wonderful new gadget, outfit, or piece of sports equipment that will bring us fulfillment. Our closets are filled. Our shelves are crowded. We keep plenty busy, trying new recipes, restaurants, and vacation destinations.

How strange it is that our hunger continues to gnaw at us. No matter how much we bring into our lives, we are soon out on the road again, looking for something better. Some tigers and cougars are especially talented at bringing in the "big game." Others only go after those targets that are smaller and slower. Nevertheless, all tigers and cougars are soon outside hunting again. Always outside; over there, somewhere else. Someone else to ease the pain, the emptiness.

How strange it is that no matter how long and difficult the hunt, no matter how willing or unwilling the objects of our desire are, we are never satisfied. Tigers and cougars are solitary, predatory creatures. My thesaurus says that to be predatory means to plunder, to be rapacious, to take, to clutch, to steal, to extort. Harsh words to describe the simple request that the world ought to be responsive to our special demands.

Someone said to me recently, "Barbara, it occurs to me that God can take better care of what I need than all the external players put together."

Talk about heresy! What you genuinely seek can be best found inside your own heart and mind and soul? Give up the hunt? But I've gotten to be such an excellent cougar. I know the paths, the watering holes, the lookouts with the best vantage points!

What would an unemployed cougar do with his or her time? Possibly, become the rarest of animals—a human being who is open, curious, and content.

You Get Used to It

How many Unitarians does it take to change a light bulb in our congregation? Answer: none. We don't change light bulbs. It is enough for us to sit in the darkness and remember the light of the past. As we honor the memory of a former brilliance, our task is to live within the confines and limitations of today.

True story. When I arrived in 1983, I was told that the lights under the sanctuary balcony didn't work, had never worked, and couldn't be fixed. It was not a big deal. We have few services in the evenings, and there are plenty of lights in that sacred space that do work.

Only our new sexton, Ron Lundin, did not believe that they were forever broken. He decided to investigate. He took off the glass plate and found a thick, dark coating of dust and dirt.

He thought, "There's no way it could just be the light bulbs, but I'll put in a fresh one, just to see what happens." And then the miracle occurred, "and there was light and it was good."

Incredulous, he changed the bulbs in the other six fixtures, and light poured forth. Apparently the bulbs had burned out in 1939, and no one ever changed them. The dust he removed from the recesses was in place when Hitler invaded Poland and John Steinbeck published *The Grapes of Wrath*. We don't know whether the seven bulbs burned out all at once or flickered off one at a time. In either case, someone decided the fixtures didn't function, and that transmitted wisdom left us in the dark.

Many years ago I faced a similar situation at the parsonage where I lived in Illinois. For five years, as I had washed dishes, I had stared out of a smudged, streaked, grimy kitchen window. Because the window had been painted shut for decades, I accustomed myself to looking through the gray film. Then along came a professional painter, and not knowing the limitations of my world, he hit the window rim with a hammer. He "unstuck it" and took out the storm windows. The panes were washed and put back. The task required a total of twenty minutes.

For five years, I resigned myself to the inevitability of blurred vision. Sometimes we settle too quickly for "seeing through a glass darkly." Sometimes the clarity and illumination we seek is close at hand. Conditions can change. Windows can open. We just need to stop believing that we already have enough light.

Early Corn

There are all sorts of ways to be a snob. One of them is agriculturally. You can say, as I have, "The only time to get good corn is in the height of the summer. The only good corn is local corn. The only way corn can be sweet and glorious is when you eat it on the day it was picked." If you believed this dogma, you'd be skeptical about tasting corn-on-the-cob in the springtime.

But in early April on an especially warm day, I was at a farm stand, thinking about how long it had been since I had tasted corn-on-the-cob. Something about the corn display made me wish I was a little more open to a broader view of the corn season. When the lady called my number, I put on my most suspicious demeanor and casually asked (more in disbelief than as a genuine question), "The corn . . . is it any good this early?"

Much to my surprise, she replied with unusual enthusiasm, "It's wonderful!"

Well, now I was in a quandary. Either follow the truth as I knew it and wait until July or fling caution to the wind, take an expert's counsel , and serve corn-on-the-cob for dinner. I chose the latter. It was an act of foolish extravagance, I thought.

That evening, I served it to my guests, with many apologies and disclaimers. All of us agreed it was at least aesthetically pleasing to see a novel vegetable on the table, but we shared very low expectations about its quality.

We were, thus, stunned to discover that the corn was delicious, some of the best we'd ever tasted. Grown in Florida and swiftly moved to Massachusetts, it was as sweet and almost as tender as the best we'd eaten out of the garden.

Jesus taught, "The harvest is ready right now, and it is abundant." He wasn't referring to corn-on-the-cob. He was speaking about grace and love. Too many of us concluded long ago that we could only experience the sweetness of grace and love under certain limited circumstances. But I suspect that life's graciousness is more extensive than we have imagined. It is closer at hand. It is available early and late. It can come in any season.

Grace and love can be found in places we've never bothered to look before. They can surprise us when we least expect them. Sometimes it's necessary to forget all our hard-won knowledge and spiritual expertise. We don't have to stay hungry. We need to find the sweetness of today.

Next!

My friend Steve claims that his philosophy of life has finally been simplified to the extent that it could be expressed in one word. "*Next!*" Whatever the challenge in his life might be, he wants to be ready to meet it. Whatever he wakes up to, whether in his professional life, relationships, errands, or health conditions, Steve wants to have the same poise and balance as a man behind the bakery or deli counter, welcoming his next customer with the friendly greeting, "Next!"

Next!

What bewildering, demanding assignment has life given me to accomplish today? What completely outrageous problem must I find a way to solve? Whether it's a leak in the plumbing, a funny noise in the car engine, or the realization that it is no longer possible to put off paying the bills, I like the idea of simply facing the task that presents itself. All that is required is an open heart, a curious mind, and a willingness to engage with reality.

There are, of course, alternative ways to view the world. One of my personal favorites is to hope each morning when I open my eyes that the day will go smoothly. (Smoothly being defined as nothing interfering with my pre-existing plans, no unpleasant delays, and especially no events that make me aware of my dependency or limitations.)

If you approach daily life with the expectation that nothing ought to interfere with your own predilections and preferences, you are likely to resist and reject much of what happens. Resisting what is real, fighting with reality, getting angry and depressed with "what is" is an exhausting and, ultimately, losing battle. Reality has a persistent way of showing up on your doorstep. You can waste a whole lot of time wishing reality were simpler, less demanding. But the ever-changing circumstances of this life keep presenting themselves to us. The critical question is "How will we respond?"

I don't have the temperament or the religious maturity to greet every challenge with peaceful composure or to delight in whatever is God's will. I don't have the unselfishness or the trust to welcome each new disruption with an optimism that declares "this too can be conquered or made workable."

But I love the image of someone behind a counter yelling out, "Next!"—determined to offer what service and talent are available when a new proverbial customer appears. As I get older, I find I must ask life's challenges to get in line and take a number! I fully expect that some of the "customers" will be difficult and some will bring a gracious blessing. Some of the changes ahead will bring astonishing new life. Some will break my heart. And when one challenge appears to have been met and fully addressed, I am confident that the next challenge is waiting in the wings.

Euripides wrote 2,500 years ago, "All is change, all yields its place and goes." Then we find ourselves face-to-face with the mystery of whatever comes next.

Appointments to Keep

I am not one for reading oracles, interpreting dreams, or divining signs. My world usually unfolds for me in a rather mundane and practical manner. However, you can get my attention by hitting me between the eyes with a two-by-four.

For instance, because of a heavy snowfall and high winds, the church roof leaked. Considering our roof covers tens of thousands of square feet, it was an amazingly small leak. One steady stream of about a gallon of water focused and limited itself to two square feet of damage. Now, where do you suppose, in our vast building, that this water landed? Certainly not in a hallway or a bathroom where it would have little effect. Certainly not in one of our large empty halls where a bucket and a mop could have easily taken care of the damage. No, it leaked right square in the middle of the minister's desk.

I have a rather large desk. On it are hundreds of dollars worth of books, piles of sermons, unopened mail, and church records. None of this was touched. Other than the blotter, which lost its life in a valiant attempt to sop up the unexpected torrent, only one item was destroyed—my appointment calendar. This calendar was chock full of appointments, conferences, sermon titles, meetings, deadlines, and commitments into the next year. There is no tool I use more frequently or rely on more heavily than this calendar. It represents for me productive work, a busy schedule, a certain order, and a comforting map of challenges and obligations that lie ahead. Now it lies curled up on my desk—matted, wrinkled, and warped. It is still somewhat legible, but so misshapen that all the information will have to be transferred to a new book.

The specificity of this leak causes me to take notice. I am shaken at the thought that the creator of roof leaks does not take my busy life as seriously as I do. I wonder whether God is as impressed with my hectic schedule, long hours, and many commitments as I am. My immediate conclusion is "apparently not."

What fills our days and nights can so easily become endless distraction. We become perpetual motion machines that never reflect on the ultimate purpose of all this activity. Having my calendar destroyed has given me pause. Perhaps it is not how much we do that matters. The spirit in which that work is done is more important. If we forget whom we serve, if we neglect to tend to the resources that give us the energy to complete our tasks, then more than appointment books get harmed. Our very lives are diminished.

As our calendars fill up and our schedules are established, may we return to the prayers and the grace that hold these structures in place.

Rank Beginner

My husband and I once gave everything we owned to a man who couldn't find his way back to where he had parked his moving van. He was our "professional" mover. Despite the fact that he was sent by a reputable national corporation, he had some sort of "directional" dyslexia. He could not read a map. He could not tell left from right or north from south. We had to point him out the front door, tell him to keep the house to his back, and turn towards the hill when he got to the end of our long driveway. Needless to say, this did not engender confidence on our part. We had just given him all of our material wealth, and he couldn't find the truck he'd put it in!

We lived in Illinois—how was he going to find Worcester, Massachusetts? Put the sun behind you as the day grows late? Keep driving till you hit the ocean and then ask someone to turn you in the direction of north?...

The end of this story is equally amazing. Without a map or directions, he got to Massachusetts. He even found Worcester. He got off at what he thought was a good exit and found our street within five minutes. On his truck was a sign that said, "This rig is owned and operated by the holy spirit." You'll get no argument from me.

At the time of our move, I enjoyed telling the story about our mover with some derision. But more and more I've come to identify with his predicament. In life, most of us travel blindly a good deal of the time. We might have a pretty good sense of where we want to go and how we'd like to live, but all the good directions in the world don't seem to make the journey much easier. We spend a lot of time feeling lost.

We learn one lesson, turn a corner, and discover there are greater challenges ahead. We master one skill and suddenly realize that a new set of circumstances demand an entirely different training. Spiritually and emotionally—and sometimes even intellectually—I feel like I'm still in elementary school. I'm always looking ahead at a staggering amount of wisdom I have yet to learn, constantly overwhelmed by my own ignorance and how far I have to go.

It's not that we aren't making some progress. I've been told that God works on us like a skilled carpenter. Once God has one side polished, God quickly turns us over onto another side, which is still rough. The unfinished side is always up, always the side we see. Even if one part of our life finally runs smoothly, we instantly become aware of another aspect that needs work.

I know some people feel that their education is behind them and that they can rest on the expertise and the talents that they have already developed. But I will keep company with other rank beginners, with the ones who often feel bewildered and lost. We rely on the holy spirit, however we define it. I like to travel with those who know that the way ahead is impossibly far, and who, nevertheless, put the sun to their backs and go forward in faith.

Worst Answer

✐

Every spring I look forward to the arrival of my *Walking Magazine* "shoe edition." In this issue, dozens of brands and styles of shoes are rated, assessed, analyzed, and recommended for different walking needs. Last year, I read about my own "perfect" shoe. It had narrow heels, extra cushioning, boxy toes, and good ankle support. I clipped the article and went to my nearest athletic specialty shop. Unfortunately, they didn't carry that model. Neither did the next six shops I visited.

I went to the eighth shoe store with low expectations. Much to my amazement, there they were! I tried them on and they were probably the most uncomfortable sneakers I'd ever put on my feet. I was stunned. These shoes had obviously not been designed with my feet in mind! I tried on three different sizes, but there was no way around it. My well-researched hunt for the perfect shoes had been a failure. I tried on a different pair, not even listed in my magazine, and they were wonderfully comfortable. I left the shoe shop with my new shoes, puzzled about the benefits of being an educated consumer. All the information in the world couldn't adequately replace the hands-on wisdom of direct experience. I suspect this is true not only of shoes but also of things far more important.

If you're like me, when your research is not providing the results you want, the next step is to do more research. In this frame of mind, I called a close friend last week with a simple question. The subject was not shoes. The subject was an intense backache. I asked him, "What can I do about the pain I'm in?"

His answer was immediate. He said, "Well, Barbara, you're just going to have to suffer."

"Suffer?" I thought. "You mean I can't dodge this, solve it, manipulate it, avoid it, fix it, make it go away, transform it? You have no information, no wisdom, no insight that can change pain into pleasure? I have to actually experience this feeling for some time to come? I'm powerless? You mean I can't talk, think, or intellectually wiggle my way out of this?"

Suffering was not the answer I wanted. Yet I could hear the truth in it. Some of life's experiences simply must be accepted. You're not supposed to enjoy them, love them, or seek them out. You've just got to survive them.

Someone once told me that a functional theology is like a comfortable pair of shoes. The world will occasionally offer to us rocky and difficult ground to walk on. Good shoes will allow you to cross over broken glass without cutting your feet. They will carry you across hot pavement without getting you burned. They'll take you across sharp rocks without bruises. This metaphysical / theological footwear will not make glass, hot pavement, or rocky terrain disappear. But good theology will give you some support, some protection, and some comfort. It will help take you the distance.

Things!

✒

Things! In corners, in boxes, hanging in closets, filling up drawers. Standing in the middle of the room, decorating walls. Where did all this stuff come from? We are in the process of moving, and the source of the current crowding is more than a casual concern. In October of 1975, I could fit everything I owned into one midsized Ford. What awesome forces have transformed my earthly goods into unmanageable proportions?

My immediate impulse was to find someone to blame. People must have been steadily sneaking things into the parsonage while I was sleeping. Over the years, little by little, through a diabolical conspiracy, someone had been smuggling objects into the manse and then quickly escaping, empty-handed. A kind of burglary in reverse, robbing me of simplicity—leaving me to polish and dust, sort and clean. They were a merciless band of importers, who left me with no space in my cupboards!

Except this was not the work of professionals. The evidence was everywhere. All these things looked familiar. We had brought this deluge of material excess onto ourselves.

Things do occasionally leave via the infrequent garage sale or spring-cleaning. But every piece of mail, all the books, clothes, plastic bowls, unused pieces of material, "bargains" picked up on impulse, and everything bought at full price or on sale—it all adds up.

The rate of inflow over output in a house is a critical figure. You must be especially wary of the "special-occasion flooding" —birthdays, Christmas, weddings. Beware of visitors bearing "things" in deceptively pretty wrapping paper. Watch out! The wrapping paper is always hiding something! Guests arrive with parcels and depart without them. Pretty soon you have a crowded future.

It happens slowly. You barely notice the subtle advance of objects, despite the omens and early warning signs. You run out of hangers; you're unable to find drawer space; you have no room on the shelves for your groceries. At first, you hardly notice. You buy a new chest of drawers. You tuck your treasures in the attic or the basement. You never think that someday, all of those three-dimensional objects will demand attention, handling, and lifting.

I have developed a radical, new, temporary rule while we are packing to move: "What comes in will have to be either consumed or carried out." I acknowledge no exceptions to this law. Eat it or take it away!

Before you turn the key in the lock of your front door, examine the parcel in your arms—be it a piece of junk mail or an antique sofa. Ask yourself, "Can I swallow this?" If not, you may awaken one day to find your possessions swallowing you.

TheRightBean.com

When children are small, parents can project an amazing amount of expectation and fantasy onto them about their gifts and potential. As you introduce them to hiking in the mountains, you can imagine them growing up to be environmentalists. With their first art course, you can see their hidden undeveloped talents. As they show strength in particular areas of academia, you can't help but wonder whether they might follow in the footsteps of your own intellectual curiosity.

An ongoing, underlying dynamic in our home is that one parent —the Dad—teaches physics and loves science, math, and technology. The Mom—me— is completely liberal arts: history, literature, psychology, philosophy, and world religions. So it was astonishing when Robert, our oldest child, announced that he was going into business for himself. Business! That is neither fish nor fowl! Neither the Mother's nor the Father's area of expertise, knowledge, or experience. But our senior in high school decided that he was going to become an entrepreneur, the founder of an on-line coffee business. He would be the middleman between a wholesale coffee roaster and the cyberspace gourmet-coffee consumer. In addition, this venture would fill the requirements for his senior research project.

My instantaneous response was, "You can't do that. You're only sixteen! And we can't help you at all. We don't know anything about marketing a product!"

And like any normal sixteen-year-old, he completely ignored my counsel. He went to banks and arranged credit. He hired classmates and friends to design a website, paying them a percentage of the profits. He obtained insurance. He bought the software and security to handle credit card purchases. He found a wholesaler and worked out prices and shipping. He took photographs for the website of his buddies sipping coffee in our living room. My role, meanwhile, was to roll my eyes and tell him, "This will never work." In the nine months that the project has taken, there have been countless setbacks. Each time, I was the one who encouraged my son to give up and move on. To his great credit, he didn't listen to me.

Recently, we got a call from a salesman, asking if Robert Merritt was the marketing supervisor for *TheRightBean.com*. We didn't tell him that the founder of the company was attending class. We didn't mention that Mr. Merritt was also in charge of publicity, purchasing, advertising, technical maintenance, finances, deliveries, and payroll.

And then, what I thought could never happen, happened. The site became fully operational. Coffee orders started to come in, and the founder of the company was smiling a lot.

Parents can be slow learners in discovering how little we know. *TheRightBean.com* has been a good spiritual teaching for at least one skeptical mother.

The children of God are meant to follow their own dreams. We are all called into the business of creating unimaginable futures.

Steppingstones

They give you fair warning when you visit Scotland. Every novel and guidebook makes direct reference to the wet and unpredictable weather. In August, we visited the Isle of Skye, one of the Hebrides Islands off the western coast of Scotland. And while it rained almost every day, the sun also shone on a regular basis. The mountains and the moors were lush, carpeted with thick, emerald-green grasses. We grew appreciative of a climate so wet that it could support such vegetation. One early morning, I went on a solitary hike into the Cullin Hills, the highest mountains in Great Britain. The trail started right outside our hotel. The drizzling air was damp and cold but the scenery was magnificent, and the trail was an easy walk through a lovely valley. The only challenge was the path. It was wide but wet! Sometimes I felt as if I were following a streambed rather than a path. All the water from the high moors on either side seemed to converge on this path. And sometimes the water pooled to form large lakes with muddy bogs on either side. The only things that made the path passable were the steppingstones. Volunteers had carefully placed rocks in close proximity to one another so that walkers could, with some degree of balance and luck, skip across the wet terrain.

Alone at 6:00 in the morning I was pleased with the first steppingstones I encountered. An hour and a half later, having benefited from the placement of hundreds of these stones, I became acutely aware of how much effort had been expended by strangers. There is something so simple and ordinary about carrying a rock and placing it where it will assist a fellow traveler. Simple stones, placed down by ordinary people, gave just enough assistance to make a journey possible. Their hard labor allowed me, and many other people they would never meet, to go deep into the mountains to experience a rare beauty. The work is not permanent. The water and weather will move the rocks, submerge them, and carry them away. Yet, it is a significant gift to bestow on perfect strangers. Of course, steppingstones do not only exist in Scotland, nor are they only composed of rocks across streambeds. The small things we do for friends and for strangers make a difference, helping them across their own streams. A kind word or a helping hand can keep us from sinking into discouragement and fatigue.

The forces of change and upheaval are powerful and inevitable. As it says in the old hymn, "Time, like an ever rolling stream, bears all its sons away." But the human spirit is a worthy match for such forces.

May you discover some steppingstones in your travels today. And may you find a way to build a path for others.

What We Require

I am one of those people who love to make New Year's resolutions. Why not create a vital, remodeled persona, new and improved? Just write down all the things you want to accomplish, all the projects you want to complete, all the character improvements you want to make, and all the skills you want to master. At the start of a new year, it seems reasonable that resolutions would carry extra momentum. January feels like an especially auspicious time to become the person I've always wanted to be. If I write it down, surely I'll be able to keep my desk neat, my home well organized, and no thank-you note will go unwritten. Surely this is the year that the houseplants and garden will not be neglected. I'll find more time to play with my kids, my friends, and my husband. I'll read more books and watch less television. I'll exercise more and eat fewer desserts.

The fantasy life contained in your average New Year's resolution is rich and sweet. It starts with the premise that thinking of an ideal self will increase the likelihood that you will be transformed. Resolutions are also aesthetically satisfying; they give the appearance of order and control. They allow you to picture yourself without flaws, limitations, or setbacks. How could the new, improved model ever feel the kind of fear, inadequacy, and need that the old self has structured its life upon?

41

But my favorite delusion, embedded in a list of resolutions, is the illogical but stubborn belief that only more effort is required for a better life. No real change of heart is needed. Just do what has never worked before, only do it more. Try harder. Work harder. This is music to the ears of all of us who try to defy gravity by pulling ourselves up by the boot straps. Some of us believe that we can earn love and approval. We think that the race belongs to the swift. No matter what Jesus said, we secretly are convinced that "the first will be first" and "the last will be last."

The word "resolution" in my thesaurus reveals the shadow side of our "best laid plans." To be resolved includes being "relentless, self-willed, and obstinate." To be resolved means "to set one's jaw, to nail one's colors to the mast, to burn one's bridges, to stop at nothing." It also means "to be rigid, inflexible, hell-bent, and like a bulldog. To take the law into one's own hands."

What I admire about religion is its stubborn refusal to accommodate these foolish illusions. Religion, while honoring human effort and inviting our firm resolve to be the best human beings we are capable of being, insists that we need to experience what it means to be loved and to receive grace. What we require will come to us. Effortlessly.

Mechthild of Magdeburg's words need to go right beside my New Year's resolutions:

42

Effortlessly love flows from God to humanity
As the source strikes the note, humanity sings.
The holy spirit is our harpist,
And all strings which are touched in love must sound.

Hoping for Good News

Whenever there is snow in the forecast, I become a weather news addict. With luck and intuition, and some physical agility with the remote control, it is possible to see the meteorological predictions on the 6 o'clock news of all three major networks. I'm fascinated to hear who promises the most total snowfall and who is forecasting more conservatively. My husband refers to all snow predictions as "The Big Lie." We've had our expectations raised so many times with promises of "six to twelve inches," only to have it all turn to rain or, especially galling, go south of us, that he no longer wishes to trust these "experts." But I continue to appreciate and get quite caught up in all the prognostication.

But circumstances beyond my control this Sunday evening caused my routine to go awry. Just at the time when all the TV weather people were making their estimates and telling us what to expect, we were in Boston. How was I to find out what they had predicted? As I was going to bed, I suggested to my husband that he could tape the 11:00 p.m. news, so that I could watch it in the morning. He pointed out that in the morning all I would need to do was to open my eyes and look out the window. The logic in this approach was hard to argue with. It forced me to confront my own love of prophecy.

Prophets are people who tell us what is going to happen in the future. In the Biblical tradition, they were the ones in the tribe with enough courage to confront the kings. They were also the moral conscience of the society. They reminded their listeners that more was going on than met the eye. They spoke of the long-term consequences of today's actions and the folly of "quick profits," and careless decisions. They made courageous speeches and upset the status quo. As a colleague recently reminded me, they rarely died of natural causes.

Prophets from long ago are appealing to modern students of history. We know how the story turned out. The empires that looked so invincible at the time would not last. The ethics that met the needs of those in power would inevitably lead to the downfall of that particular regime. Now we hear the ancient prophets and know that they were speaking the truth. But back then, the prophets were dismissed as madmen, troublemakers, negative thinkers, and deluded fanatics.

Most of us are fascinated by what people tell us about the future. We're hoping they will tell us good news. We desperately want to believe that "things will go our way." It is not at all surprising that there has always been a booming business for false prophets—individuals who tell us what we want to hear. The best weather forecasters, in my book, are not the most accurate. I like the ones who promise the largest accumulations. But these extravagant meteorologists rarely apologize for missing the amount of the actual snowfall by a country mile.

It will be a good day when religious people say, with greater frequency, "I don't know." Like the weather forecasters, we can't be sure.

New Worlds

Professional conferences are profoundly influenced by location. I try to go to a retreat in Little Compton, Rhode Island, once a year because the inn where we stay is situated right on the ocean. I find the chance to walk on the beach to be every bit as beneficial to my spirit as any conversation among colleagues.

This particular conference was held in February. The high temperature hovered around twenty-two degrees. A strong wind blew off the ocean; one could call it "brisk." But the sun was out, and wild swans glided on the pond. The crashing surf was beautiful, and I felt very grateful to have an hour to hike along the beach.

I was surprised to find that people were swimming in February. Actually, surfing. They had on wet suits, head to toe. Dressed in my down parka, hat, gloves, fleece scarf, and extra warm boots, I passed one young man who was dripping wet with a broad smile on his face. I asked him whether or not he thought it was a little cold to be in the water. He grinned back at me and exclaimed, "All the best waves are in the winter! This is my favorite time of year to surf."

He sounded like my husband. Our family was recently doing some winter hiking in the White Mountains. On an especially beautiful trail, looking down at a roaring brook covered in icicles, he said, "Hiking is much more fun in the winter than it is in July. There are no bugs or crowds. After you've warmed up from exertion, the outside temperature cools you down. And the views are spectacular when the leaves aren't out."

On our first day of winter hiking, we came across large, fresh bear tracks in the snow. The next day the temperature had dropped to ten degrees, with a bitter windchill. When we stepped out of the car and were hit by the force of blowing snow, I wondered whether or not winter hiking was such a great idea. Then we reached the waterfall at the top of the trail. Thousands of icicles glistened in the sun. It had snowed several inches the night before, and creation looked as beautiful as anyone could imagine.

Who says you can't enjoy the beach in January? Who told us that mountains in the winter are only for skiing? We tell ourselves. We shut our doors and look out the window and see only gray or brown. We believe that nature will only be accessible when spring returns. It's not true.

I suspect we often see the world more narrowly than it actually is. We say, "There's no way," when in actuality we have several ways to meet the challenge. If we go exploring past the barriers we believe are impenetrable, we may discover new worlds. People can walk joyfully across frozen fields. Those of us who hope for more light and clarity might find a treasure hidden in the darkness. In the hardest of seasons, we may come across a grace and a splendor that will transform our lives.

In Your Eyes

Someone recently told me that he thinks God shows up after one dies in whatever form will bring the most comfort to the individual soul. If you're a Christian, God will come for you in the form of Jesus. If you are a Buddhist, God will appear as the Buddha. If you are an atheist, God will flood your heart, soul, and mind with the love, truth, and meaning that you longed for so fiercely in the world. If you are a cat, God will come as a cat. If you deeply loved someone who has died—and heaven could only mean a reconciliation with that person—then God will come for you as that individual. A musician would be welcomed by magnificent music, the artist by beauty, the poet by sublime lyrics. It makes a certain intuitive sense that, according to the limits of our own perception, we will see what is real in different ways. Here on earth, human beings perceive truth and reality in their own idiosyncratic ways.

I am drawn to Dan Ladinsky's translation of a poem by Hafiz about seeing God. The poet wrote that when God wants to make his presence known on earth, he makes his appearance in "the love and playfulness in your eyes."

Your eyes? My eyes? Is it possible that sometimes we are not even aware that we are bearing witness to a power greater than ourselves? When we love one another, when we have enough trust and gladness, we are often playful. Light-heartedness, enthusiasm, and animated exuberance are so powerful that they allow us to see God in each other.

Some look for God in temples, rituals, and scripture. Some find the holy in a sunset or in an autumn leaf. But the greatest reassurance I have experienced is when God takes human form. God is made real in the human eyes that bless us with their love and laughter. The way we look at one another has the power to make God's presence known on earth.

Controlling Chaos

✍

My husband, the physics teacher, receives a weekly magazine called *Science News*. A recent cover story, in bold letters, riveted my attention and I snatched it: "Controlling Chaos." Now, that's a practical theology! My hopes soared. Here, in concise scientific prose, was the potential solution to my checkbook, my desk, my attic, my basement, my schedule, and possibly the junk drawer in the kitchen.

I took notes as I eagerly read the text. It said,

Just as small disturbances can radically alter a chaotic system's behavior . . .

Have the author's children also been sick?

. . . tiny adjustments can also stabilize its behavior.

Tiny adjustments? Why didn't I think of that? What tiny adjustments?

I read further.

The success of this strategy for controlling chaos hinges on the fact that the apparent randomness of a chaotic system is really only skin deep.

Is the scientific community sure about this? Have they ever seen my desk, or the toy room?

Beneath this chaotic unpredictability hides an intricate but highly ordered structure.

This is not obvious to the casual observer of my life.

This is akin to balancing a ball on a saddle, the ball won't roll off the saddle's raised front or back, but continual adjustments are needed to kick it back into position, as it begins rolling off the sides.

Continual adjustments! Now I'm beginning to think scientifically. What continual adjustments?

We don't avoid the chaos: We stay in the chaotic region.

Yes, I do that!

You don't need to have a deep theoretical understanding of what's going on. All you need to know, in effect, is the shape of the saddle.

Shape! All I need is to understand the shape of my chaos! What shape?

And then, eureka!

The author writes that the way to keep chaos under control is *by a constant stream of nudges*.

Aha! I now have scientific proof that my intuitive reaction to chaos works. Nudge it! Don't disturb or organize it. Nudge it!

The article has a very upbeat ending. It claims that chaos is not something to be avoided. Due to the flexible and dynamic nature of chaos, "chaos may offer a great advantage."

I breathlessly await further scientific breakthroughs in this area. Meanwhile, I'll go nudge a few papers on my desk.

Love Knows You

When my youngest child was a baby, the sweetest part of my day was putting David to sleep. At fifteen months he had a demanding schedule. There were toilet paper rolls to unravel, dressers to empty, bookshelves to clear, trash baskets to dump on the floor, papers to tear, pans to bang, books to redistribute throughout the house and office, pigeons to chase in the park, food to massage into his hair, a brother's toys to covet and fight for, and a considerable collection of bright and educational playthings to utterly ignore. By 7:30 at night little David was stumbling through the house like a drunken sailor: cranky, exhausted, and too tired to walk in a straight line.

But when I warmed a bottle of milk and he climbed up into my lap, the transformation was nothing short of miraculous. He would start to drink his bottle, and all the tension and agitation would melt away from his face. As he nestled into my arms, the frantic energy and the frustration disappeared. His body relaxed. He started to smile and hum to himself, and in a few minutes he was asleep. As the look of peace came over him, I found myself feeling wonderfully peaceful as well.

Most little children find a place of comfort, safety, nourishment, and love in their mothers' and fathers' arms. It's the place to go after a long hard day, a reality they can trust. Again and again, they return to this sustaining relationship.

Independence is fine. There will be more mischief and explo-
ration tomorrow. But babies seem to instinctively sense how
important it is to recharge their batteries and to allow someone stronger to take care of them.

I suspect that meditation and prayer are motivated by the
same instinct. In our prayers, we are "nestling in" with reality,
adopting a stance that declares we trust what is "out there"
and what is "inside." In moments of meditation we assume a
certain confidence, a faith that what is, is ultimately friendly,
capable of supporting our life, and able to restore us to our
full strength and potential. In a posture of receptivity and
dependency, we allow for the possibility that a power greater
than ourselves will hold us, feed our starving souls, and give
us peace.

Our best prayers are when we can simply turn our faces in
the direction of love. One of my favorite Buddhist prayers
reads in part:

*You may come to this Love, for a few seconds, then go away and do
whatever you will.*

God's Love is unchanging.

*You may deny the power of Love, to yourself, then curse God to anyone
who will listen.*

God's Love is unchanging.

You may become the most despised of creatures, then return.

God's Love is unchanging.

53

Go where you will, do whatever you will, stay however long you will, and come back.

This Love is unchanging.

No matter what befalls, no matter what you become, Love awaits you always. Love knows you and serves you. God's love for you, in a changing world, is unchanging.

No-Fault Volcanoes

Once upon a time, in the early 1900s, a beautiful resort was thriving in northern California. Located on a large and lovely lake on the north side of one of America's most beautiful mountains, Mt. Shasta, the Grass Lake Lodge appealed to all who loved swimming and boating and beautiful scenery. What could possibly go wrong?

Someone had the bright idea that the marina could attract even larger boats if only they could dig the channel in the lake a little deeper. The best technology of that time for opening up the ground was dynamite. So they set off a few explosions.

What no one apparently understood was that Grass Lake was created by volcanic activity. The geological construction of the large shallow lake consisted of a top solid hard shell covering a lot of loose volcanic pumice. The man-made explosion cracked the hard shell and had the same effect as pulling the plug in a bathtub. All the water in the lovely lake quickly drained away, never to return.

The resort quickly went out of business. Now, in the grassy plain, the only "vacationers" are some interesting species of birds. It has also become a rest stop by the side of the highway where you can have a picnic and read the story of the lake that disappeared.

I can't imagine what the hotel manager must have felt as he watched the water vanish in front of his eyes. He might have gone into "attack mode," blaming the engineers and explosive experts who had come up with the stupid idea to deepen the marina channel. But what good would it do to criticize or accuse, or to assign blame and condemn the perpetrators? The water would still be gone. And no trial determining who was right and who was wrong would ever bring the water back. Neither would a severe assessment of who was intelligent and who was a bumbling idiot change the nature of the new reality. No more water meant no more lakeside resort.

When circumstances change, it is time to roll up our sleeves and do some problem solving. It's time to use whatever creativity and resourcefulness we have. "Whose fault is it?" becomes not just an academic exercise but a waste of time.

In all of human history, mistakes are made. We say things we wish we hadn't. We do things we regret. One option is to condemn all humanity. A better alternative, to my way of thinking, is to figure out what to build next.

Perhaps a Nap?

There are all sorts of ways to serve God, to affirm the life force, to survive the challenges of existence. On this day, I wish to praise the "moss piglet," whose proper name is "tardigrade." Moss piglets have a phylum all their own. They are smaller than a comma and cannot be seen by the naked eye, but these little critters are remarkable.

Karen Brammer, a colleague in Saco, Maine, made me aware of moss piglets. She described a microscopic gummy bear that moved slowly, "like a sleepy park animal overturning trash cans." But these little bear-like water creatures do more than lumber through time and space. They can survive almost anything, almost anywhere.

A Google search yielded a rich harvest of information. A tardigrade's normal habitat is damp: moss, roof gutters, fungus, algae, and forest litter. They live in oceans, fresh water, hot springs, mountaintops, and rain forests. They have plump bodies, four pairs of legs, and tiny little claws. I imagine the tardigrade as looking like some kind of a weird combination of armadillo, tree sloth, Michelin tire man, and space alien.

I find the way they handle stress most inspiring. When conditions change, as conditions always do, these small animals curl up in a ball (called a tun) and take a nap! They have been called the ultimate slackers, veritable "damp, tiny couch potatoes." They lose their water, sort of become like instant coffee, and hibernate till the environment is more hospitable. This hibernation, called cryptobiosis, allows their metabolism to drop to .01 percent of their normal rate. In this near-death-like state, they become the ultimate contenders in evolution's game of "most likely to succeed." When moss piglets take a nap, they're ready to take whatever is coming their way. They can survive heat of 304 degrees Fahrenheit and freezing temperatures of minus 328 degrees Fahrenheit. They can withstand pressures six thousand times greater than sea level, a pressure that crushes most of their tougher bacteria cousins. You can dry them out on a piece of moss and tuck them away in a dusty museum for one hundred years, and a drop of water will bring them to life. They can survive radioactive radiation, X-rays, vacuums, acids, and solvents. Their exoskeleton appears to be almost impenetrable. One scientist has voted the tardigrade "most likely to be able to survive a trip on a meteorite," so space travel cannot be discounted. All of this marvelous talent to survive comes with a cost. As the moss piglet ages, it gains weight, develops age spots on its skin, and grows more hair.

Fossil remains of the tardigrade go back 100 million years, and they have the optimism of a creature that's been around that long. They know that the earth is a tough place, with occasional ice ages, volcanoes, droughts, and floods. So they have adapted accordingly—they take naps when they need to.

I am astonished. And inspired. I hear the couch calling ever so sweetly.

Migrating Souls

Unitarian Universalists have gotten one thing completely right. We are right about "diversity." We say that all of God's children are welcome. We don't ask that everyone believe the same thing or walk the same walk. We affirm the unique truth of each individual's experience. We have a deep trust that each soul will come to truth in its own time and in its own way.

I know this theology is right because it corresponds so clearly to the reality observable in the natural world. God is obviously deliriously in love with diversity. Nature is a symphony of diversity. Not only are no two snowflakes alike, neither are two human faces precisely alike. Especially as winter comes to New England and the trees shed their leaves, you can see that no two trees have the same arrangement of branches. The same species of tree, planted at the same time, receiving the same light, fertilizer, and wind, spread their branches to the sky in unique and unpredictable ways.

A marvelous documentary entitled *Winged Migration* finally drove home for me just how right our insistence on diversity is. You might think that birds migrating—sometimes just a few hundred miles, sometimes over 12,000 miles from the Arctic to the Antarctic—would all flap their wings in a similar manner and arrive according to the same schedule. You would be wrong.

Close camera work reveals that some of the ducks have to flap their wings so strenuously and rigorously that they look like they will have heart attacks before they have crossed the lake. Other birds, notably pelicans, are so adept at riding the wind currents that they look like they float rather than fly. Some birds are graceful, especially the storks—when they walk they have the grace and elegance of ballerinas. Some birds land on water with a smooth and seemingly effortless agility. And then other birds seem to just hope for the best in their rapid descent as they crash-land, dropping their legs like stumbling clowns.

The grouse spread their wings in ostentatious display. Other birds hide themselves with camouflages, seeking the protection of invisibility. Some of the mating dances of the birds are breathtakingly beautiful. Others are comical or bizarre. Some birds fly five miles high. Some birds, like penguins, can only waddle on the ground. Penguins are great swimmers, but as they emerge from the ocean, the waves can crash them against the rocks.

Each species has a preferred habitat as vastly different as arctic fields, steep cliffs, rooftops, and Amazon treetops. These birds have everything in common, and almost nothing in common. True, they all migrate. But they do it in their own way, on their own schedule, in their own fashion.

Remember these extraordinary birds the next time you find yourself in profound disagreement with another soul who sees the world quite differently than you do. If you are having a day that appears to be going awkwardly, slowly, and with far too many harsh winds, snowstorms, or collisions with rocks, take heart. You are not alone. Every soul is trying to go home.

A Gratuitous Duck

✍

Maybe I don't get out much. But I have always heard the word gratuitous associated with "gratuitous sex and violence" in movies I don't want to see. Other negative connotations include a gratuitous insult or a gratuitous humiliation. The definition I always assumed was that gratuitous meant unnecessary, arbitrary, indefensible, senseless, and unjustifiable. Until I purchased a gratuitous duck. On my day off, a friend and I were visiting an art gallery in Brattleboro, Vermont. I was not intending to buy a duck. I did not need a duck. I was not looking for a duck or any other sculptures of farmyard animals.

But there that duck was, with soulful eyes. Standing a full sixteen-inches tall, made with a hand-carved wooden body, a metal neck and head—a handsome piece of primitive folk art. While it clearly belonged in the mallard family, the colors were a beautiful blend of gold and green. I was surprised to find out that the duck was not very expensive. Completely on impulse, caught up in some whimsy I did not understand, I purchased said duck, intending to place it in the foyer of our home. But this duck gives me such delight that it is now sitting in our living room. Every time I see it, I smile.

It has been hard to explain to my family why I felt the need to purchase this rather large, multi-colored, aquatic bird. And then, someone told me it was a "gratuitous duck." I assumed initially that this was an insult, a way of saying that the purchase had been frivolous and indulgent. But no. I was introduced to the other meanings of the word gratuitous.

Gratuitous comes from the same root as *gift*, *pleasing*, *gratitude*, and *grace*. Latin: gratis. Something that comes to us as a free gift, a spontaneous and unmerited, unlooked for and unbidden gift is a "gratuitous gift." Theologically, grace is often referred to as "gratuitous grace."

I had not earned this duck, hoped for it, or searched for it. I wasn't even conscious that I wanted it, let alone needed it. Yet, there it sits, in a central place of my living room, offering a blessing that partly has to do with beauty and partly to do with something more mysterious.

The universe offers many uninvited gifts. Some seem unnecessarily harsh and capricious. I'm never happy with such "gifts"—I resist them, resent them, wail against them, and fiercely wish they had not found their way to my address.

And then other gifts are sheer grace, absolutely gratuitous, in the best sense of the word. A smile from a stranger, the first warm day of spring, a flower coming up through an old icy snowdrift, an email from a long-lost friend, a word of encouragement from a colleague. I just need to focus on the truth that grace shows up in surprising ways.

I have a duck to prove it.

Unitarian Universalist Meditation Manuals

✒

Unitarians and Universalists have been publishing prayer collections and meditation manuals for 150 years. In 1841 the Unitarians broke with their tradition of addressing only theological topics and published *Short Prayers for the Morning and Evening of Every Day in the Week, with Occasional Prayers and Thanksgivings*. Over the years, the Unitarians published many more volumes of prayers, including Theodore Parker's selections. In 1938 *Gaining a Radiant Faith* by Henry H. Saunderson launched the tradition of an annual Lenten manual.

Several Universalist collections appeared in the early nineteenth century. A comprehensive *Book of Prayers* was published in 1839, featuring both public and private devotions. Like the Unitarians, the Universalists published Lenten manuals, and in the 1950s they complemented this series with Advent manuals.

Since 1961, the year the Unitarians and Universalists consolidated, the Lenten manual has evolved into a meditation manual.

2006	*A Guest of the World* Jeffrey Lockwood
2005	*For All That Is Our Life* Helen and Eugene Pickett, Editors
	Admire the Moon Mary Wellemeyer
2004	*We Build Temples in the Heart* Patrick Murfin
	Consider the Lilies Stephen M. Shick
2003	*Walking Toward Morning* Victoria Safford
	How We Are Called Mary Benard and Kirstie Anderson, Editors